Under an Ancient Sky

Selected writings
by
John M. Ketterer

Avid Readers Publishing Group

Lakewood, California

The opinions expressed in this manuscript are those of the author and do not represent the thoughts or opinions of the publisher. The author warrants and represents that he has the legal right to publish or owns all material in this book. If you find a discrepancy, contact the publisher at www.avidreaderspg.com.

Under an Ancient Sky

All Rights Reserved

Copyright © 2010 John Ketterer

This book may not be transmitted, reproduced, or stored in part or in whole by any means without the express written consent of the publisher except for brief quotations in articles and reviews.

Avid Readers Publishing Group

http://www.avidreaderspg.com

ISBN-13: 978-1-935105-83-1

Printed in the United States

Contents

Green Tea..1
A Higher Heart..39
In the Glow of Now..65
Under an Ancient Sky..93
Points of Light...157

Green Tea

Honor every moment by being present.

One
drop
of truth
touches
everyone.

Not only must
we be present
every moment

we must also
be present between
the moments.

I

breathe in

the quiet

then I unfold

my quiet

the sacred silence

circles around me

I am neither here

nor there

but everywhere.

Dip your brush

into life's ink

quick

tarry not

your response

to the fleeting moment

and

the heart's desire.

We try to

hold on

to the moment

cannot hold on

must live the moment

must feel the moment

must BE the moment.

When you

do not know

your true self

there is no foundation

light winds

can scatter your

deck of cards

distractions

are many.

Circumstances

seem to limit

your options

take a breath

choose large

from the

celestial menu.

We are all

going home

some fast

some slow

time is irrelevant.

All wars
are solved
from within
the heart.

Stillness

unfolds

all

that

needs

to be unfolded.

When
you are in
the deep woods
there is a
deep silence

and a
deeper
you.

Sometimes

our lives

are brief sightings

like fireflies

in the grand fabric

of life

waste not

each moment.

We explore
the infinite

we dive into
the unknown
and the mystery

we dive into
ourselves.

As
I enter
into nature
beauty is
everywhere

it sails
my soul
into the heavens

then
I am
everywhere.

Give me
the trees
in a green
forest

the sun
that treads
across the water

the silence
in the garden

the moments
of no thought

a sip
of tea

the warmth
of your hand

the peace
in our hearts.

Keep your
vision pure

keep your
vision clear

keep your vision
of the true you.

Change
breaks
illusion
shell

new
life
is
created.

Moonlight

stillness

oneness.

Body tired

smell

jasmine

flower

refreshed.

Sky unfolds

mind quiets

I unfold.

A dull meal

friend

arrives

everything

tasteful.

Time
drags

enter

passion

time vanishes.

People have secrets

use layers of
protection

please unfold
natural self.

War rages

chaos everywhere

ladybug
has normal day.

Tattered souls
   make a
       pilgrimage

connect to
   the Divine

reborn.

Life goes on

    who can define it?

we can only
    imagine it.

Crack in

old concrete

flower

slowly emerges

loving intention.

F rantic
    schedule

suddenly
    butterfly
        appears

freedom
    flutters.

Green

summer forest

is everywhere

more than a color

the breath of now.

Many different statues

each made from same clay

oneness.

You offered

an orange

how sweet

it was

how sweet

you are.

Beyond the gate

a call from
the unknown

louder and louder.

Truth

rings

true.

Silence . . .

a powerful
teacher.

A Higher Heart

The

heart

is

the strongest

medicine.

Deep down
we all share
the same heart.

The heart

threads the way

through the duality

the drama

the fear

and

the forgetting.

The heart
takes us deeper
into who we
really are.

The mind

is finite

the heart

is infinite.

We unfold

our future

moment

to moment

by our desires

and what is real

in our hearts.

We

are navigating

in the illusions

of the mind

the heart

is our one

true compass.

Hearts ignite

and in turn

ignite other hearts

the universal heartbeat

becomes louder and louder

the heart grid

grows and grows

Love touches all.

We need

flexability

of the soul

do not

be crushed

under the weight

of circumstances

changes or towering

emotions

do not be drained

by these things

because life is

ever created

within you

the abundance

is within you

ask your heart

and it will

tell you so.

All
mysteries
are solved by
the heart.

The heart
is the divine
messenger
from the soul.

Do not

be burned up

by fear

feel

the burning

of the heart.

Don't
be a stranger
to your own heart.

The mind

has many questions

that in the end

only the heart

can answer.

The heart says
to be happy

the mind says
if such and such
happens then happiness
will manifest

the heart
does not set
conditions.

We
get inundated

swept away

by the contents

of our minds

how will it feel

when we are

swept away by

the ecstatic streams

of the heart?

We are all
in each other's
hearts

we are all
in each other's
hands

we are all
bonded together
by love.

As the heart
expands
so does your
infinite love.

Listen

to the song

in your

heart

it will

strengthen

your

soul.

Gather
your precious
dreams

use these
as blueprints
for the world
you want to see

let them
flow outward
from your
inner essence

let them
play and shimmer
in the light

let them
dance with your
heart.

The
whole universe
is available to you

every moment
every second

let in the ones
that speak to
your heart.

Everything happens in your heart first

then you see it with your eyes.

The
only perfection
you will find
is in your heart

everything
is perfect there.

The heart has
the keenest eye
the deepest eye
the eternal eye.

In the Glow of Now

Come
lay down
in my heart

let's enter
the gentle streams
of love that flow
into grand oceans
of bliss.

When
your eyes
sparkle
my heart
dances

when
you smile
I know that
I am home.

Expect me

in your dreams

expect me

in the subtle moments

between breaths

expect me

to arrive

like a sweet

summer wind

expect me

to curl up

in your intimate

thoughts

expect me

always.

Your

immense love

radiates outward

and affixes like

golden sequins

to my every thought.

Let's

be lightning bolts

that strike deep

into the dark night

and light up the

still spaces with

intense flashes

and thunder.

You have
very bright eyes

some say
that they glow
in the dark

all I know
is your eyes
light my way.

You are

my recipe of choice

you are enfolded

into my life

in infinite layers

of sweetness and

joy.

Look into
the face
of love

look into
the eyes
of love

let it
pull you
into bliss.

On
that small
wooden boat
under the shadow
of the sail
your eyes
appeared as
ancient dormant seeds
which instantly found
fertile soil
in my heart
and as we set sail
over life's
mysterious waters
we knew
our journey
was on course
because our
internal compass
was set to
true love.

Dance
with me

leap into
my heart

join with me
in celebration
of all that is
and yet to come.

Let the night

be still

except for your

unfolding presence

which I enter into

with my unfolding

heart.

There was

a stranger

in my dream

a stranger

so sweet

so kind

we could exchange

laughter and

split atoms that

made the space

explode with

intimacy.

We
are like bookends

sometimes

separated by

many volumes

sometimes

by a scant few

and sometimes

face to face

with no words in between.

Tell me
what touches
your heart
and let me
touch there
also.

Come

    thrill me with your divine presence

    and your infinite breath of life

    let your divine love

    pulse and ebb through my life

    so that I may float in

    a sea of endless imagination

    let me also hear your

    divine words that are everywhere

    let me catch them

    and tune into the map of

    all consciousness so

    I can glide and revel in

    every moment.

Let me be

the shrine

that you bring

your soul to

and let me grant

that all your

prayers come true.

Let's marinate
our love in
the sweet juices
of eternity.

Keep me
in your heart
as I do you

from there
no shadows
can exist

from there
the view is infinite

from there
you will feel
like flying
and
if you fly
take me with you.

You inspire

my heart

and then you

open it

all your music

rushes in

all your

sweet notes.

You are

the presence

that overlooks

my day

you break into

my thoughts

and we ride

off into sweet

landscapes

of intimacy

then you vanish

so that once again

life's mysteries

are popping up

all around

which demand

my focus and

courage

yet

I am secure

in knowing

that you will

come again

to unfold

a deeper

sense

of love.

Tell me
when you see
the light behind
all light

tell me
when you feel
the source
of all love

tell me
when you know
there is love
and nothing else.

You arrived
like a flowing
cosmic mandala
gently bringing
a glow to my heart
like a newly
created galaxy
in my life.

Go directly
to LOVE
and I'll meet
you there.

Let's get close

let's remember
how it feels
to be in the rain

let's remember how it feels
to open up
like a flower

let's remember
all the times
that love poured
through us.

You move
through my life
like a glowing
radiant truth
that has no
limits.

Under an Ancient Sky

We all have

our version

of moonlight

yet

we all draw

from the same

moon.

Light the flame
within you

care not
if the brightness
be too bright
for others

care not about
their stares
and judgement

light the flame

brighter and brighter
higher and higher.

Are you
stalking life
or living it?

There is only
ONE HEART
shared by
ALL.

Greatness
is the grace
of being who
you really are.

Someday
we will shed
our fears
and sparkle
like dancing
energy reflections
on a forever changing
mysterious sea
of consciousness.

The waterfront
of the soul

entering into
the very depths
of beingness

passing through
the walls of fear

riding the heart waves
to core essence

a vastness so deep
it humbles all.

We all

want magic

in our lives

we need

to remember that

we ARE magic

Divine Magic.

Love
is your token
on the bus to
bliss.

Let only
your love
define you.

We are always
opening packages

unraveling

the mystery

the unknown

the threads

of excitement.

The infinite
expresses itself
in an infinite
number of ways

the infinite
entertains itself
infinitely.

The
first dance
is with oneself

the inner dance
of creation

next
we can dance
with the world.

We all have

friends in

high places

very HIGH PLACES.

We all
have our unique paths
that weave
and intersect
and gain speed
with all other paths

together
we blaze across
an infinite sky.

Sometimes
we think that
our story
is insignificant
compared to life's
immense canvass

yet
without each
unique story
the canvass
is incomplete

so
spread your
vibrant colors
with passion
upon the canvass of life

ask not

if your expressions

are valid

for only

you are you

and only

you know

what's in your

heart.

A quiet place
with no sense
of urgency
no pounding of
the brain

the moments unfold
and linger as
sweet memories

sometimes they
come and go
like the wind

there is no time
only profound
movements of existence

the moments
rise like skyscrapers
into the vast blue

higher views

become available

one moment

then another

view

upon

view

forever.

You are

the missing link

you are

the secret ingredient

you are

the infinite moment.

What opens

the heart

or what

closes the heart

this is

our crossroads

to love

or to fear.

Deep down inside
we know what
we are doing
and who we really are

discovering
and living from
this point of existence
is crucial
and is our
task at hand

from there
we have a
commanding view
of life
and all the love
we can imagine.

Everyday
we need to make
a pilgrimage to
our core self
our core truth.

Some say

that love is

just around the

corner

actually

there are no

corners because

love is all around.

With compassion
we can establish
intimacy
and with intimacy
everything we need
can be revealed.

We love

to hear

the songs

of others

also

we need

to hear

and create

our own song

when all songs

are being expressed

and heard

the world will

be in balance.

Sometimes
we drift off
to faraway places

we spin awhile
in small eddies
along unknown shores
then we are released
like leaves floating
down a stream

we become
transitioning clouds
in suspended sculptures
that lift the heart
from heavy attachments below.

Everyone

wants it

their way

this is

only possible when

everyone lets

all others to also

have it their way.

Imagine yourself gliding on the wings of perfection.

Our imagination
lights up
the world.

We all want

larger lives

however

we are already

immensely large

we are

the source

of large

we are

infinite.

We need

to rise above

the mental trenches

and walk among

the true riches

of earth

we need

to soar

with our soul.

Ancient axioms

and truths

are being unraveled

and unveiled

before us

we reconnect

to old friends

together

we lift

the crystal glasses

of clarity.

Embrace
your life
as your joy
as your creation

love it
nurture it

sail it
like a kite
in the winds
of abundance.

Sometimes
we wake up
in unfamiliar circumstances
and things have changed

flashing transformers
circle our minds

greener pastures
beckon to our eyes
and fear vanishes

the mystery pulls
our imagination
to new shores

we set sail
and the wind
catches the
unfolding moment

we are free.

Many are trying
to navigate within
the structure of
the mind

much easier
to sail in
the sea of
the infinite.

We all need
healing

when something
has been broken
big or small
then or now
seen or unseen
quiet or loud
we seek wholeness
we seek the love
that can heal

love has many forms
many doors
many faces

let your truest feelings
guide you there.

We all

have times when

we fall apart

we are spun

outward into

the world of confusion

and imbalance

sometimes dark landscapes

of unrest and bitterness

appear

we seek

to gather up

our loose ends

and make the

pilgrimage back to

our core center

the center

that is true

for us

the inner castle

of peace

with an unlimited

view of love.

We are all

dreaming

whether awake

or sleeping

such fine dreams

such fine imagination

such plots

and circumstances

such textures and colors

dreams within dreams

all traceable

to the first dream

the dream of creation

and the dream to BE.

We sail willingly
into the tapestry of wonders
caught up in the
glowing delights
and the mystery
of it all

we search
for the secrets
while the maker
of the tapestry spins
greater and greater
wonders

we search yet
all the time
WE are the secret

our true nature
our true selves.

Let's laugh

the cosmic

laugh

let's dance

the soul

dance

let's taste

the sweetness

of truth.

If
we climb
to the rooftop
of our beingness

we will
be able to see
the vastness
of who we
really are

we will be
in awe of
our true
infinite self.

The tapestry of life
weaves and unweaves

moments coalesce
and then are gone

when love strikes deep
it brings bliss

when removed
the wounds bring
pain
yet we invite
the piercings
again and again
until no wounds appear
and only the
sweet kisses
of eternity remain.

The greatest challenges can also bring the greatest gifts.

One day

I became so full

of love

that I forgot

to say my prayers

on that day

I became

my prayers.

The universe
is listening to
your thoughts.

Make a commitment to your passions.

There is

no limit

to the universe

because there is

no limit to

the imagination.

We explore
the infinite

we dive into
the unknown
the mystery

we dive into
ourself.

The

infinite

now

an

epic tale

always in progress.

Do the things
that make you
feel alive

and ensure
that those things
do not make others
feel less alive.

I want

to be everything

for you

but in the end

I can really only

be myself.

Wake

up

to

LOVE.

We all have

our castles

of truth

with spectacular

views of creation.

When love
is suppressed
twisted or
thwarted
all manner of
upsets and
imbalances
can manifest.

It's

an illusion

that love

comes and goes

that some

have it

some don't

the truth is

that love is always

present

and everyone

has it

Love...

one size

fits ALL.

No one

can tell you

what is in your heart

or what lights you up

only you can

only you are you.

We are

like

flames

flames of existence

which need air

to burn brightly

we are the flames

God is the air.

Some of us

don't color

within the lines

we go beyond

the lines

we surrender

to the unexplainable

we unfold

the spontaneous

we laugh away

the viels

we soar into

the unknown

we sleep

we dream

we create

we chase our tails

we glow with delight

we soar.

We
are all
in the process
of reconnecting
to our true source
our true heritage
our true home
our infinite self.

Points of Light

Don't

fly over

your life

get down

and walk

every step.

Be passionate about your passions.

Cut your ties
to beliefs
that bind
and to beliefs
that blind you
from the truth.

Life is everywhere

which part of it
that is set in motion
for you depends
on your desire.

What kind of dots are you connecting?

There is only
one story
with an infinite
number of chapters.

Instead of
believing in reasons
why you can't
do something
start believing
in reasons
why you can.

When
love speaks
louder than fear
we need to listen
the loudest.

The amount
of clarity present
in one's life
is directly proportional
to one's appetite
for truth.

Rather than going out and face the world perhaps it's more fruitful to go out and create your world.

One
cannot
think
one's way
into
happiness

one
has to
feel
one's
way.

We are out

chasing mysteries

we are out

chasing secrets

perhaps

we are out

chasing our

own tails.

A snowy
white winter
extends out in all
directions and
covers everything

in the same way
let your joy extend
out in all directions
and cover the world.

We endeavor

to know things

from the inside out

we need

to apply this same

procedure to

ourselves.

Sometimes
we go deep
into our story
and forget that
it is just a story

sometimes
we become afraid
of losing our story

we forget that
we can create
another story with
another title.

A tiny
drop of water
from the ocean
contains the essence
of the entire ocean

the ocean of oneness.

Perhaps

we create

mysteries

so we can

go about solving

them?

If
you dreamed

your way into

something that

you do not prefer

then dream

your way out

change the dream.

It seems

that life

has to be

very complex

otherwise

everything would

unravel

and the mystery

the truth

would be revealed

too easily.

If you know
who you really are
then nothing can
darken your light
or separate
you from you.

We
are all keys
on the same
master key ring

each key opens
a vital unique door

and collectively we
open all doors
that exist.

Feelings
run deep

follow the
currents to
the source
and bathe them
in the light

if the feelings
are emboldened
they are true

if they vanish
in the light
they are not true.

We listen
for the inner
quiet
voice

the voice
that rings true

all we have to do
is listen

there can be
many distractions

yet that voice
is waiting in
the stillness.

When
love knocks
at your door
it's best
to open it

then
you will see
a sky on fire

you
will feel
a flaming heart
that can burn brightly
in the rain and
wind and darkest night

a heart
that is intimately
linked to
the eternal flame
of love.

For eons

we have been

dazzled

by the outer world

now we are

on course

to be dazzled

by the inner world

which is the source

of the outer world.

We all

make waves

sooner or later

we must ride them

so it's better

to make waves

that take us

where we want to go.

We crave

the familiar

the known

yet

if overly

obsessed upon

the familiar can

limit our growth

we also need

to explore the unknown

the unfamiliar.

Every moment

we are

on a path

there are

many options

we always have

the power of choice.

Sometimes
it's necessary
to take hold of
the tiger's tail

sometimes we are brave
and we ride the tiger

eventually
we can be
the tiger.

Do not
look forward to
being who you
really are

say "hello"
right now.

Don't let your fears or doubts define you.

We keep asking questions until in the end we answer them for ourselves.

Sometimes

we flow with

the current

sometimes

we have to

push through

the current

and sometimes

we need to

get out of

the current

and observe.

We
can never
know everything
because everything
is constantly
being created.

A brave new world

needs brave new thoughts

brave new hearts

and an immense love

to pave the way.

You don't know what you will think tomorrow until that moment arrives.

Sometimes
we are boxing
with our own shadow

fighting with ourselves

sometimes
we are fighting
with the truth.

You know more than you think.

We all have

our inner journeys

of light and dark

of love and fear

of the known and unknown

of change and security

the drama unfolds

life unfolds

the journey unfolds.

Peace
is brought about
by knowing that
THEY are a part
of you.

We
stand upright
in the constantly
changing circumstances
in life by knowing
and being who we
really are

this gives us
inner balance
that keeps
us whole

then we have
grace and flexibility
in the complex
energies all around

we can have
focus and presence.

In a way
one has to be
completely vulnerable
to completely live
one's life.

Together

moment by moment

thought by thought

we create the universe

around us

it's dynamically alive.

We are spectators of our own imagination.

In the end

you will have

everything you need

because you

are the end

and the beginning

you are endless.

Sometimes
it's necessary
to go ahead
and anoint yourself.

We anxiously
look beyond ourselves
and eventually
arrive within.

Hopefully
we have not
developed
higher and higher
technology
to communicate
lower and lower
thoughts.

The
biggest secret
in the universe
is who we
really are.

We
all bathe
in the
eternal light

we are always
in its presence

there is no
separation.

On
the road
to clarity
there is no
dead end

there is
only you
reinventing yourself
moment to moment
thought to thought.

The infinite
is very much
alive

it's the living
lightning of now
which spawns
unlimited truths
which are highly
dynamic and
consciousness shifting

we exist
in a sea
of creation

and like

the flame

that must

have air

to survive

and burn brightly

we must keep

the presence

of the infinite

within us.

Each
one of us
is an unfolding
masterpiece.

When
we know
who we really
are

then there
will be a
foundation
to create a
world we
desire.

We play
in the finite
world

but our home
is in the
infinite.

Perhaps our biggest challenge is to decide to live in a miracle.

All our

precious souls

are illuminated

and fill every corner

of the past

present

and future.

We are on the path
to truth

yet truth is not
some faraway place

truth is all around you

truth is in you

live each moment.

We cannot escape
from who we
really are

yet we do not
know fully
who we are

perhaps this is
the ultimate
mystery.

Each moment

is a unique

interaction

with life

moments

change

moment

to

moment

life is not

static

we are

constantly

creating our world

by our thoughts

desires

intentions

life streams

are generated

we are all

masters in

different roles

of consciousness.

Fear
and the unknown
can be opportunities
to know yourself
more fully
and to bring
yourself into
wholeness.

Love
yourself

explore this
whole heartedly

Although
we can imagine
limitations
we are
in our essence
unlimited.

We create

our own

personal truth

within the great

ONE TRUTH.

Live

every moment

as if your life

depended on it

because it does.

It seems

that sometimes

we cleverly

hide ourselves from

ourselves.

what

part of you

is hiding now?

Don't compromise

with who you

really are

this is not

negotiable.

www.ingramcontent.com/pod-product-compliance
Lightning Source LLC
Chambersburg PA
CBHW061429040426
42450CB00007B/972